Hank
AND THE Kitten

Story by Ruth Dudley

Pictures by Louis Darling

Originally published in 1949
Cover illustration by Nada Serafimovic
Cover design by Robin Fight

Once there was a little puppy named Hank. He was white all over except for a black patch across his back and a brown spot over one eye. His tail was short, and it stood up straight and perky.

He was a cute little pup. He should have been happy. But he wasn't.

Hank had a kind master named Dick. Dick always kept fresh water in Hank's pan. He always remembered to feed Hank on time. He brushed Hank and washed him and kept him clean.

So Hank should have been very happy. But he wasn't.

Hank was unhappy because one day Dick brought home a little lost kitten. She was a pretty little black kitten with white paws and a white bib.

"Isn't she a cute little kitten!" said Dick, cuddling her in his arms.

Dick put the kitten on the floor. The kitten liked Hank. She rubbed against Hank's legs.

She went "Pur-r-r-r-r-r."

Hank did not like the
kitten to rub against
his legs. He did not
like the kitten to go
"Pur-r-r-r-r-r."

"Woof, woof!" barked
Hank at the kitten.

"Now, Hank, be good!"
said Dick. "Be nice to the
little kitten."

"Woof, woof!" barked
Hank and ran outdoors.

The kitten loved Hank.

She followed him outdoors. When Hank ran and played, the kitten ran and played, too.

The kitten loved to eat from Hank's dish. She loved to drink from Hank's pan of water. She loved to rub her little black head against Hank and frisk between Hank's legs. But that made Hank cross.

"Woof, woof!" he barked.

When Hank went for a walk with his master, there was the kitten scampering after them. She ran up trees. She dashed under their legs.

Dick laughed. But Hank stuck his nose in the air. He didn't like it.

When Hank lay down on his little bed, the kitten curled up beside him. Right up close to Hank she curled.

"Pur-r-r-r-r-r," she sang, happy as could be.

But Hank was not happy.

Hank grunted and moved over as far as he could. But the kitten only stretched nearer. Hank got up, yawned unhappily, and walked away. He went to a far corner and flopped down there.

But the kitten thought this was fun—a brand-new

game. Her bright yellow
eyes watched Hank—
watched him stretch way
out, his head on his paws,
and fall asleep.

Then the kitten got
up, too. She yawned and
arched her back in a great
big stretch. She walked
over to the corner and
flopped down, too, right
beside Hank, as close to
him as she could get.

"Pur-r-r-r-r-r," she sang,

happy as could be, right in Hank's ear.

Hank raised his head. He glared at the kitten and yawned again, making a very unhappy noise. But the kitten didn't mind. She just cuddled closer than ever. She liked the feel of Hank's nice soft, warm body.

"Pur-r-r-r-r-r," she sang, happy as could be.

But Hank was not happy.

Hank tried to find secret places to sleep. Once he crawled under his master's bed—way, way under, so no one could find him.

But the little kitten found him. Her bright yellow eyes peered under the hanging bedspread. Her long white whiskers stood out in great excitement. The kitten thought Hank was playing

hide-and-seek. SWISH!
Under the bed she slid,
pouncing at Hank.

Whiff! Her little white
paw batted Hank playfully
right on the nose. Tag!
You're it!

Hank woke up with
a jump. When he saw
the little black kitten, he
groaned. Then he rolled
over, turning his back.
But the kitten didn't
mind. She crawled right up

on Hank and flopped down, clear across Hank's body.

"Pur-r-r-r-r-r," she sang, happy as could be.

But Hank was not happy.

The next day Hank went outdoors. He hid in a patch of weeds in the warm sunshine. He closed his eyes. No one would find him now or interrupt his dreams!

First, he dreamed he was chewing on a nice juicy

bone. Then he dreamed he was eating a big piece of steak. Then he dreamed his master was making him some soup. It was boiling and boiling on the stove. He could hear it plainly.

Suddenly he awoke with a jump. There was the little black kitten! She had her head on his chest.

"Pur-r-r-r-r-r." She was singing right in his ear, happy as could be.

But Hank was not happy. He was very cross indeed. And when the little kitten reached up and began washing Hank's face— washing and washing with her rough pink tongue— well, that was just too much. Hank jumped up rudely and ran.

Hank just did not know what to do. Try as he would, he could not hide from the little black kitten. Try

as he would, he could not frighten her away. And Hank did not want the kitten. He did not want her to follow him around. He did not want her to eat from his dish or drink from his water pan or rub her head against him or frisk between his legs.

Hank did not want the kitten to curl up beside him when he slept. He did not want to hear her

go "Pur-r-r-r-r-r." He certainly did not want her washing his face with her rough pink tongue.

And most of all, Hank did not want the kitten to follow him when he went for a walk with his master. Hank liked to walk proudly, his head held high. Then people stopped to admire him.

When the kitten came along, she ran between his legs and tripped him

up. People did not stop to admire him anymore. They laughed at the little black kitten instead.

Hank wished a great big dog would come along sometime and chase the kitten way up a tree—so high she could never come down.

And that is just what happened. That very thing!

One day when they were walking, a great big dog came along. He chased the

little kitten way up in a tree. Way, way up in a tree.

Hank's master was busy talking to someone. He did not see what had happened. Hank was the only one who saw.

That evening Hank had everything all to himself. He had his own dish of food. He had his own pan of water. He had his own little bed. He stretched way out on his bed. There was

no one to bother him. There was no one lying across his stomach. There was no one batting his nose or washing his face with a rough pink tongue. There was no one going "Pur-r-r-r-r-r."

Hank should have been very happy. But he wasn't.

It began to get dark. Hank lay on his bed with his head on his paws. His eyes were open, and he was watching his master.

Dick was looking under chairs and tables. He was calling, "Kitty, kitty, kitty. Here, kitty!"

But no kitten came. Hank kept his head on his paws and his eyes on Dick.

His master opened the door. "Here, kitty, kitty, kitty," he called. But no kitten came.

Hank stretched way out on his nice wide bed and tried to go to sleep. But

he couldn't. He heard his master calling and calling outside.

"Here, kitty, kitty, kitty! Come, kitty!"

Hank tried very hard to go to sleep. But he couldn't.

Dick came back in and closed the door. He looked at Hank. "Where is she? Where's the kitty?" he said.

Hank saw that his master looked very sad. And all at once Hank thought of

the poor little black kitten way up in the tree. Out in the dark. Out in the cold. Hungry and frightened and shivering. Hank blinked his eyes.

He felt sorry for the poor little kitten. His bed felt big and lonely. He had thought he would be happy, but he wasn't.

All of a sudden, Hank jumped up from his bed. He ran to his master and

barked, "Woof, woof!" He took his master's trousers in his teeth and pulled him toward the door.

"What is it, Hank?" asked Dick. "What are you trying to tell me?"

His master opened the door, and Hank dashed out as fast as he could. Dick ran with him.

When Hank came to the tree, he stopped and looked up and began to

bark. There, way up—way, way up—was the kitten.

"Ma-a-a-a-a-o-w!" the kitten cried.

The kitten looked tiny and black and frightened. She did not know how to get down.

"Good boy," Dick said. He patted Hank's head. "Good old Hank! Wait here. Stand guard!"

Dick went away and came back with a man

who carried a long, long
ladder.

"Now we'll get you
down," Dick said to the
frightened black kitten.

"Ma-a-a-a-a-o-w!" said
the kitten.

The man leaned the
ladder against the tree
and climbed up until he
could reach the kitten. He
brought her down and
handed her to Dick.

Dick carried the kitten

home in his arms.
Hank walked proudly
beside him. He could
hear the kitten going
"Pur-r-r-r-r-r."

Back home Hank wagged
his tail at the kitten. He
let the kitten eat out of
his dish. He let the kitten
drink out of his water
pan. He even jumped and
played when the kitten
frisked about his legs. And
when Hank went to sleep

on his bed, the kitten was there, curled close.

Dick was happy.

"Good boy!" he said and patted Hank's head.

The kitten was happy, too.

"Pur-r-r-r-r-r," she sang and cuddled close to Hank.

Hank was very happy indeed. His bed did not seem big and lonely anymore. His tail went

thump, thump, thump against the pillow.

More Level 2 Books from
The Good and the Beautiful Library

A Wolf in the North Woods
by Heather Horn

Brave Little Ruby
by Shannen Yauger

Seth and Beth
by Jenny Phillips

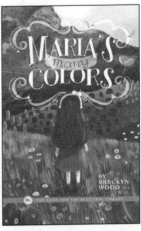

Maria's Many Colors
by Breckyn Wood

goodandbeautiful.com

Level 3 Books from
The Good and the Beautiful Library

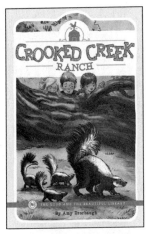

Crooked Creek Ranch
by Amy Drorbaugh

Mother Penny
by Gertrude Robinson

Sammy
by May Justus

David and the Seagulls
by Marion Downer

goodandbeautiful.com

Printed in Canada
1.0FRL229